The Ayatollahs and the MEK
Iran's Crumbling Influence Operation

By Lincoln Bloomfield Jr.

UNIVERSITY OF
BALTIMORE
College of Public Affairs

Copyright © 2019
University of Baltimore
College of Public Affairs
1420 N. Charles St.
Baltimore, MD 21201-5779
www.ubalt.edu

Printed in the United States of America.
First edition. July 2019

ISBN-10 (Paperback): 0-578-53609-9
ISBN-13 (Paperback): 978-0-578-53609-5

ISBN-10 (e-book): 0-578-51732-9
ISBN-13 (e-book): 978-0-578-51732-2

Library of Congress Control Number: 2019908751

Library of Congress Cataloging-in-Publication Data

The Ayatollahs and the MEK: Iran's Crumbling Influence Operation

1. Iran. 2. Intelligence. 3. Middle East. 4. Terrorism. 5. History.

BOOK DESIGN: Auburn Associates, Inc., Baltimore, MD.
PHOTO CREDITS: Cover background photo: © iStock, Nic Taylor;
cover inset photo: © AFP/Getty Images

ABOUT THE COVER: *Iranian security forces on motorcycles threaten opposition
protesters during clashes in Tehran.*

Former Senior Leaders in National Security, Counter-Terrorism and Law Enforcement comment on "The Ayatollahs and the MEK"

Michael B. Mukasey, U.S. Attorney General, 2007–2009:

"The surest way to kill a lie is to pour truth on it. In this monograph, both methodical and compelling, Lincoln Bloomfield Jr. — who served in national security positions in both the State and Defense Departments of three presidents — kills at least six lies about the MEK, an organization of Iranian dissidents dedicated to replacing the theocratic tyranny of the mullahs in Tehran with a republic committed to democracy and gender equality. These accusations range from the bizarre — that the MEK promotes an extremism rooted improbably in both communism and Islam — to claims of violence against Americans and the Iranian people, and suggests that the laziness of journalists who will not examine these canards critically is exploited by regime sympathizers in the United States. This essay should be read by anyone concerned about the security of the United States and the world."

General James L. Jones, USMC (Ret.), U.S. National Security Advisor, 2009–2010; NATO Supreme Allied Commander, 2003–2006; and Commandant, U.S. Marine Corps, 1999–2003:

"Once again, Ambassador Bloomfield has brought clarity and truth to the forefront of one of the most embarrassing episodes of our involvement in Iraq. Our "non-action" policy was one which inflicted great damage to our national moral authority on human rights issues, tacitly enabling the overt (but under-reported) massacre of hundreds of innocent men and women on the orders of both the Iraqi and Iranian governments, all in the misguided and false hope that the persecution of the MEK would curry favor with the regime in Iran. For anyone who continues to believe the lies regarding the only opposition group Tehran truly fears, Ambassador Bloomfield's essay is necessary reading. For our diplomats and elected leaders, it should be required reading."

Louis J. Freeh, Director, Federal Bureau of Investigation, 1993–2001:

"There was no credible factual or legal basis for putting the MEK on the FTO list in 1997. Unfortunately, it was a misguided foreign policy gimmick by the Clinton Administration to curry favor with the Tehran regime, and to pave the way for some fantasy U.S.-Iran 'rapprochement'. In addition to murdering 19 U.S. Airmen at Khobar Towers in 1996, and relishing its role as the largest state exporter of terrorism, the mullahs never had any intention to act as a lawful nation state. Conversely, the MEK saved countless U.S. military lives in Iraq, and has been thanked and praised by America's senior military leaders."

Foreword

By Ivan Sascha Sheehan, Ph.D

In the years following the 1979 revolution in Iran, hundreds of students and faculty were killed, victims of a brutal campaign to silence dissent, stifle academic freedom and impose uniformity of thought. Thousands of other students and faculty suffered brutality, torture and detention for "propaganda against the system," "participating in illegal gatherings," or "insulting" government officials, i.e., exercising rights guaranteed under international law to freedom of speech, freedom of association and peaceful assembly. Tens of thousands more had their university educations or careers upended and were forced into exile. This assault on academic freedom did not stop in the 1980s, but has instead become a principal feature of the contemporary Iranian regime…

In totalitarian societies, power is maintained in part by the control of memory and reinvention of the past. While all societies promote a collective history, totalitarian states tend to advocate a single authorized version.[1]

IN THE PAGES THAT FOLLOW, Ambassador Lincoln P. Bloomfield, Jr. presents breaking revelations and documents compelling evidence that the Islamic Republic of Iran's organized opposition, the Mojahedin-e-Khalq (MEK), and its parliament-in-exile, the National Council of Resistance of Iran (NCRI), have been falsely portrayed in Washington for years. A careful examination of the facts supports this conclusion and tells a very different story than the one authored by Tehran and too often echoed in Washington.

With this publication, Ambassador Bloomfield directly and authoritatively refutes the charges brought against the regime's organized resistance and the underlying narratives that have sustained them. *The Ayatollahs and the MEK* explodes the regime's disinformation campaign and brings a fresh perspective to the Iran policy conversation. Contrary to the falsehoods circulating in Washington, the MEK has served as the principal opposition to clerical rule since

---

[1] Sheehan, Ivan Sascha, *Iran's Assault on Academic Freedom, The Hill*, September 11, 2016

the 1979 Revolution. The organization, the key element in the broader coalition of resistance groups within the NCRI, has only grown in strength, popularity, and political prowess since this time.

Ambassador Bloomfield — a Distinguished Fellow and Chairman Emeritus at the Stimson Center with a sterling reputation in Washington — has extensive experience with Iran policy, accrued while serving as a senior national security official in five U.S. administrations. In 2011, as a non-attorney advisor at a prominent Washington law firm retained by Iranian-Americans seeking the removal of the MEK and NCRI from the U.S. roster of foreign terrorist organizations, he conducted an independent assessment of the terrorism allegations made against the groups and published a detailed report demonstrating that the most credible sources available did not back up the allegations. The report was translated into French and Farsi and the U.S. Department of State submitted it as a source material in the court case reviewing the MEK-NCRI terrorism listing, which was subsequently lifted by the Secretary of State. Meeting with Parliamentarians and exiled resistance members in Europe, Ambassador Bloomfield furthered his knowledge of the group and its history, testifying about his findings before the U.S. Congress.

In 2013, in my capacity as an evidence-based counterterrorism scholar, I collaborated with Ambassador Bloomfield in the publication of a study on the history of the MEK. We methodically examined all of the alleged terrorist activity over the group's fifty-year history using the most reliable references. The resulting picture was very much at odds with the image and specific allegations believed to be true by many in the U.S. policy community.

And yet, almost six years later, we regrettably still encounter journalists, think tank experts, former U.S. officials, and Iran policy watchers who accept Tehran's narrative rather than objective facts and falsely tag the MEK and the NCRI with a terror label.

The publication of the enclosed monograph is an acknowledgement that the unfortunate myths peddled by Tehran in Washington and around the world persist. Unsurprisingly, the regime's claims have become even shriller in the wake of the years long countrywide uprising that has engulfed the regime and the continued efforts by the organized resistance to topple the mullahs from within.

In late December 2017, mass protests sprang up across the Islamic Republic, starting with the city of Mashhad. Initially focused on economic grievances, the movement quickly took on a much broader political tone with participants chanting "death to the dictator" and demanding a government that accommodates dissenting voices. Less than two weeks later, as regime authorities struggled to stifle the movement, Supreme Leader Ali Khamenei publicly attributed the uprising to the MEK, stating that the opposition had planned for months to popularize the anti-government slogans and facilitate the protests' rapid spread to over 140 cities.

Unable to deter or contain the unrelenting, pervasive, and geographically widespread protests in 2018, the IRGC gunned down scores of protesters in the streets, arrested more than 8,000 citizens, and detained, tortured, and executed others. In a speech before the 2018 U.N. General Assembly, President Trump acknowledged these atrocities and described the Iranian people as the longest-suffering victims of the clerical regime and underscored the separation between the Iranian government and the Iranian people.

The amplification of efforts initiated by Iran's own resistance community in 2019 — particularly those undertaken by the MEK/NCRI — have consumed the clerical rulers and prompted a fresh examination of the mullahs' hold on power. The April 2019 designation of the Iranian regime's Islamic Revolutionary Guard Corps (IRGC) as a Foreign Terrorist Organization struck a significant blow to the foremost global state sponsor of terrorism. The Federal Register, the official journal of the U.S. Government, now clearly identifies all IRGC forces — including the Qods Force, Basij Organization, Aerospace, Navy, and Ground Forces — as foreign terrorist organizations, with all of the privileges and penalties pertaining thereto.

Fearful that their reign may collapse, Iran's leaders have stepped up their influence operation by repeating tall tales in prominent newspapers and by making dubious assertions about the regime's opposition. We shouldn't be surprised. As I noted in a recent article:

> For decades, Tehran's theocratic rulers have gone to great lengths to make inroads in Western media outlets once notable for upholding commitments to journalistic independence. These efforts have been so successful that many such organizations are now threatened from within by assets — often disguised as journalists — portraying Iran as the victim of U.S.-led interference and even a looming war. These instruments of propaganda are used to demonize the regime's opponents at key moments and stave off basic freedoms that would cause the regime to collapse like a house of cards.[2]

---

[2] Sheehan, Ivan Sascha, Tehran's Influence Operations a Threat to Journalistic Independence, *Townhall*, December 6, 2018

One might have hoped that the corrective message reflected in the pages that follow would be unnecessary in our nation's capital on such a consequential national security issue as policy toward Iran. Nevertheless, the message is needed and indeed long overdue. I am hopeful that Ambassador Bloomfield's assessments will contribute to an informed, principled consensus on how best to deal with the regime in Tehran. Such an outcome cannot arrive soon enough.

The ability to challenge conventional wisdom or call out the Iranian regime's falsities is a freedom not afforded scholars or public servants in Iran. In fact, repeated assaults on basic freedoms are a routine feature of Iran's contemporary political landscape. That Ambassador Bloomfield would be blocked from acknowledging the basic facts presented in this monograph were he to seek its publication in Iran is a further indication of its importance here in Washington.

Tehran's belligerence coupled with the regime's repeated dismissal of U.N. Security Council resolutions can be expected to inch the international community toward more assertive policies. But to chart a new course for Iran policy, the U.S. will need to convince its allies to line up behind a new vision for Iran — one ideally characterized by a free, democratic, and pro-Western society that rejects dictatorship, whether illustrated by the rule of the deposed Shah in 1979 or the ayatollahs today.

A fuller embrace of the democratic aspirations of the Iranian people must necessarily begin with efforts to dismantle Tehran's influence operation and correct the factual record vis-à-vis the architects of freedom in Iran — the MEK and NCRI. Ambassador Bloomfield's evidence-based counterintelligence assessment of the Iranian regime's influence operation is an important step in this direction and an opportunity I hope bipartisan U.S. officials will embrace.

Ivan Sascha Sheehan, Ph.D.
Executive Director | Associate Professor
School of Public & International Affairs
College of Public Affairs
University of Baltimore

The Ayatollahs and the MEK
Iran's Crumbling Influence Operation

By Lincoln Bloomfield Jr.

FOR FOUR DECADES, Iran's ruling elite has kept the Washington establishment focused on the bright, shiny object of its terrorist activity, augmented in recent years by its rush to develop nuclear enrichment and related capabilities. U.S.-Iran relations have wavered between episodes of heightened tension and periods marked by hopes for rapprochement with the clerical regime. U.S. diplomats, absent from Iran since the traumatic hostage crisis, have searched for a path back to normal relations with this regional power of 80 million people with its rich, 2,500-year heritage. Nuclear proliferation specialists, long hopeful of restraints on "rogue" state nuclear weapons programs, have mostly welcomed the 2015 Joint Comprehensive Plan of Action (JCPOA). Others have focused on Iran's internal repression and malign external behavior, advocating more pressure on the regime. With President Trump openly endeavoring to dismantle President Obama's legacy, including by withdrawing in 2018 from the JCPOA, the Iran conversation has been further colored by partisan sentiments.

Consensus on Iran policy is therefore elusive. Was the Trump Administration wise or unwise to withdraw from the nuclear deal? Could moderate elements in Tehran reform the regime such that Iran would no longer threaten the security of others? Was Secretary of State Mike Pompeo's demand for 12 major concessions by Iran reasonable? Should the U.S. steer clear of escalatory actions, accept that this regime is here to stay for the long term, and seek an authoritative channel that might return both governments to the negotiating table? Will the recent designation of the Islamic Revolutionary

Guard Corps (IRGC) as a Foreign Terrorist Organization (FTO) advance or complicate U.S. efforts to curb Iranian threats? Is the Administration trying to provoke a war with Iran? Policy experts are divided on what kind of relationship the U.S. should want with Iran's rulers, and how to pursue it.

On one Iran issue, however, one is far more apt to hear a similar view from establishment experts, namely that the 54-year-old resistance group known as the Mujahedin-e Khalq — MEK — and the Paris-based umbrella organization known as the National Council of Resistance of Iran (NCRI), are unworthy of mention in polite discourse of Iran policy, and in any event entirely irrelevant to the subject of Iran's future. By implication, any Americans who consort with this group or speak positively about it are, to one degree or another, ignorant, reputationally compromised, and deeply misguided.

What was, for many years, a 'fringe' topic that surfaced occasionally in Iran policy commentary has lately become a predictable, if not principal, feature of think tank discussions on Iran. A spate of condemnatory articles about the MEK has appeared. They repeat a litany of defamatory allegations familiar to Iran-watchers: the MEK are and always were a terrorist organization, harboring a violent Marxist ideology (incongruously combined with Islam); they murdered several Americans in Tehran in the 1970s; they helped seize the American Embassy; they initiated a campaign of violence against the new post-revolutionary government under Ayatollah Khomeini; and when Saddam Hussein attacked Iran, the MEK took up Iraq's side in the war against their own people — an act of unforgivable treachery, compounded later by the MEK's alleged role as a strike force within Saddam's brutal campaign to suppress the Shia and Kurdish uprisings following the Gulf War of 1991. Accused misdeeds aside, the group is also frequently referred to as a cult whose members suffer cruel deprivations and human rights abuses. Their devoted support of NCRI leader Maryam Rajavi and her husband, Massoud Rajavi (who has not been seen publicly since 2003) is, accordingly, indicative of an absence of free will.

Every one of the foregoing assertions and characterizations about the NCRI and MEK is false or deceptively misleading. Only their endless repetition by the Tehran regime's propaganda and intelligence services has caused many in the West to assume they are true. Corroborating evidence is non-existent, fabricated or distorted in ways that for years went critically unexamined in the U.S. and elsewhere. Today, credible evidence contradicting these allegations and defamatory claims is abundant, but has been disbelieved or disregarded.

Iran's rulers have routinely demanded that the U.S. and allied governments treat the MEK as a shared enemy, as the price of their cooperation. It is no small accomplishment on Tehran's part that Washington has become so thoroughly indoctrinated with spurious narratives manufactured and promoted for the convenience of a regime striving to hold onto power without a popular mandate.

The above will be met with disbelief, even flat denial, by many in the U.S. who are morally certain that the MEK and NCRI, listed by the U.S. collectively as a Foreign Terrorist Organization from 1997 to 2012, should never have been removed from the list. Yet in truth, they should never have been on it. And the question national security experts need to be asking now is how the establishment — including a national security bureaucracy that signed off on ever-more incorrect and embellished *Country Reports on Terrorism*, year after year, about the MEK — could have come to believe so much that was, and is, entirely untrue. It is hard to conceive that U.S. interests are better served by willfully continuing to ignore a body of relevant information about Iran's contemporary political history, particularly information that the rulers in Tehran know all too well.

The Final Verdict on Alleged MEK Terrorism

Start with this fact: no member of the NCRI or MEK, spanning now three generations since its inception in 1965, has ever been prosecuted or convicted of terrorism by the U.S. or any country governed with due process under the law. Fidelity to this singular truth would have precluded a vast portion of what has been published about the MEK in the U.S. and other countries for many years. Better late than never.

Now consider the translated words of French Investigative Magistrate Marc Trévidic in April 2011, concluding an 8-year investigation of the NCRI's and MEK's entire dossier, pursuant to the 2003 roundup and arrest of Maryam Rajavi and 159 other NCRI members and affiliates in France — an operation launched by the Chirac government at Tehran's request, involving 1,300 police, the largest police operation in French history: *"The dossier does not contain any evidence indicating an armed activity that would intentionally target civilians. If such evidence were available it would confirm terrorism and would annul any reference to resistance against tyranny....Knowing that the dossier is devoid of evidence for charges...to show that they committed acts of criminal association to prepare for terrorist activities and provide financial assistance to a terrorist organization, we order the dismissal of charges, of this charge against persons named above, and against anyone else."*

Every member of the MEK, numbering well over 3,000 men and women then resident at Camp Ashraf in Iraq, was individually interviewed and screened in 2004 by a 70-person U.S. inter-agency task force, including officers from the FBI, the Intelligence Community, and the Departments of State, Defense, and Homeland Security, with the outcome that, as the *New York Times* reported on July 27, 2004, "there was no basis to charge any member of the… opposition group…with violations of American law" for activities at any time in the past.

Senior U.S. national security leaders responsible for protecting against all terrorist threats worldwide from the time the MEK was first placed on the terrorism list have made clear that at the time of the FTO designation, and thereafter, no material evidence of MEK or NCRI terrorist activity ever came to their attention, either from the State Department or the intelligence agencies. After initiating the terrorist designation in 1997, the Clinton Administration explained to the press, on background, that this had been a political gesture to the Khatami government in hopes of moderating Tehran's behavior and perhaps engendering better U.S.-Iran relations. The FBI Director learned of the MEK's terror listing only after the fact, and had not been consulted for any comment or review. At the same time, the Secretary of State requested the FBI to cease its surveillance of Iranian 'sports teams' in the U.S., despite having been advised by the FBI that Iranian Ministry of Intelligence and Security (MOIS) agents were embedded in these teams. The FBI disregarded the Secretary's request.

Time and again, with country after country, the Tehran regime demanded that foreign governments treat the MEK and NCRI as terrorist organizations. Time and again, Western governments accommodated these requests, deputizing their own criminal justice bureaucracies in service to the world's most lawless and destructive state actor, seeking to suppress its exiled political opponents. Families were kept separated; for fifteen years until 2012, law-abiding Americans minimized contact with their Iranian relatives out of fear that they would face prosecution. In no case was a terrorist designation of the MEK or NCRI instituted on the basis of a confirmed act of MEK or NCRI terrorism.

Not only the French prosecution, but three other major court cases in the UK, the EU and the U.S., found senior jurists visibly irritated that their respective constituent governments had failed to produce any credible evidence, classified or otherwise, meriting the designation of the MEK or NCRI as terrorist organizations despite doggedly pressing to maintain the designations. The U.S. Court of Appeals for the District of Columbia Circuit patiently challenged Secretary of State Hillary Clinton to point out the specific evidence on which she might justify a U.S. designation; there being none, she ended the group's terrorism listing, faced with a Court deadline that would have forced her hand. The State Department acknowledged that the U.S. Government had no evidence of violent activity by the MEK for the prior ten years.

Neither the NCRI members in France and other western countries, nor the more than 3,000 men and women of the MEK, now resident in Albania after being relocated there from Iraq in 2016 by the UN, had any foreknowledge of, or role in, the assassination of Americans in Tehran in the 1970s. Nor did they help plan or participate in the takeover of the U.S. Embassy and seizure of 52 American hostages, notwithstanding their outspoken criticism of the U.S. for having supported the Shah. These historic crimes have been thoroughly researched, and allegations of the MEK's responsibility have been debunked, most credibly through the words of the actual perpetrators in both cases, who considered the MEK to be rivals for influence in pre- and post-revolutionary Iran.

Observers are free to applaud or criticize the NCRI and MEK. But for American foreign policy specialists to continue in 2019 to refer to them as terrorists or perpetrators of crimes against the U.S. is either to display ignorance of the group's actual history despite many authoritative reviews and clarifications in recent years, or to reveal a bias informed by considerations other than a commitment to respect and disseminate the truth. This is troubling, because the corrected history has undeniable policy implications, and the Washington debate on Iran is impaired so long as important truths remain obscured behind a Berlin Wall of regime propaganda.

Massoud Rajavi — The Non-Person Most Feared by the Regime

Like Lord Voldemort in the Harry Potter series, Massoud Rajavi, a member of the original MEK and its leader after the Shah fell, has somehow been assigned the status of "he who must not be named" in discussions of Iran. Inside the Washington Beltway, conversations may end abruptly with the very mention of his name; the reaction is visceral. Why? Most Iran-watchers know little or nothing about Massoud Rajavi other than the defamatory caricatures promoted by the Shah and later the ruling mullahs. Of one thing they are certain: his persona is radioactive in regime circles.

For U.S. policymakers, his is a story worth knowing. Massoud Rajavi represented the greatest challenge to Ayatollah Khomeini's claim to power after the revolution. He was the only candidate banned by Khomeini from running for President in the 1980 election (and, scholars claim, was marked for death along with his supporters by Khomeini via a hand-written *fatwa*). The core issue had nothing to do with terrorism, the Iraq war, or Marxist ideology. Released from prison in January 1979, Rajavi was the sole survivor of the original MEK's lead organizers — all executed seven years earlier — and assumed the leadership role.

MEK supporters had been among Khomeini's entourage during his Paris exile. While some were skeptical of Khomeini's intentions, they hoped, like so many of their countrymen, that the charismatic Ayatollah shared their aspirations for a new leadership in Iran free from foreign influence. As *Time* magazine reported, Khomeini's departing words in Paris as he returned to Tehran from 14 years of exile referred to *"the struggle for freedom of conscience and the way of democracy desired by all clear-minded Iranians."* Yet within days of his triumphant return to Iran on February 1, 1979, Khomeini began imposing religious restrictions, particularly on women. He extended discrimination against women in sports, granted men the unilateral right to divorce, and revoked the law on women's social services. On March 7, Khomeini imposed the compulsory veil on women employees, a diktat carried out within the Army by a 31-year-old Hassan Rouhani. Now Khomeini wanted Rajavi's endorsement of his proposed new constitution. He invited Rajavi to visit him in Qom in the fall of 1979.

That meeting changed Iran's history, as Massoud Rajavi told Khomeini he could not endorse the totalitarian mandate — *velayat e faqih*, or 'guardianship of the Islamic jurist' — which was and remains the centerpiece of Khomeini's constitution. To anoint the new Supreme Leader (by virtue of being considered the embodiment of the 12th Imam of the Prophet until such time as he reappears on earth) with the absolute temporal power to override any law or act of government would, Rajavi judged, nullify the revolution, instituting dictatorship at the very moment when millions of Iranians had been led to expect long-denied participatory democracy. No less important, Rajavi and the MEK correctly anticipated that by enforcing a retrograde interpretation of Islam, one entirely at odds with the MEK's emphasis on freedom as the focal point of religious belief, Khomeini's constitution would constrain their own practice of

Islam, which they took to be entirely compatible with an enlightened, educated lifestyle for women and men alike, equally empowered with political agency and guaranteed rights. Massoud Rajavi's refusal to endorse fundamentalist dictatorship not only challenged the political legitimacy of Khomeini's audacious power grab, but disputed the religious legitimacy of his claim to a divine mandate, the very core of the regime's power. It still does.

Rajavi came from a prominent family, and received a degree in political law from Tehran University, where he also taught English. He was known for his erudition and intellect. His brother, human rights activist Kazem Rajavi, held doctoral degrees from universities in Paris and Geneva, and was made Iran's Ambassador to the United Nations in Geneva following the fall of the Shah. They had three other brothers, including Saleh, a cardiologist in France, Ahmad, a British-educated surgeon, and Hooshang, an engineer in Belgium.

Massoud Rajavi was, in the latter part of the 1960s, among the youngest of the university students meeting in secret — the Shah having cracked down on political dissent — to draw lessons from the nationalist uprisings in Algeria, Cuba, Vietnam and elsewhere. They debated strategies to unseat the Shah and bring about a more just society uncorrupted by either the imperialist west or the godless Communists to the east. Not long before, Kings Farouk and Faisal II had been deposed in Egypt and Iraq; Idris of Libya would fall in 1969. Iran's own nationalist moment had been aborted with the 1953 CIA coup that restored the Shah from exile. The legacy of deposed Prime Minister Mohammed Mossadeq resonated with these students, followers of (later Prime Minister) Mehdi Bazargan's Freedom Movement. From its formation in 1965, the MEK's purpose was to pursue social and political change, not to wage acts of terror. The Shah's security services knew nothing of its existence for six years.

In August 1971, many leading members of the MEK, including Massoud Rajavi, were arrested in sweeping raids by SAVAK, the Shah's secret police. A month later, when others in the group who had evaded arrest were discovered plotting to tarnish the Shah's image of invincibility by knocking out the power during the planned 2,500-year Peacock Throne celebration, more MEK members were arrested. By the end of October, nearly all of the true MEK members, among them the twelve most senior organizers including Rajavi, had been detained. Sixty-nine were put on trial. The poised, defiant final statements of some of these young Iranians, as the Shah's military tribunals pronounced their death sentences, were smuggled out and created a sensation among Iranian student populations inside and outside the country, particularly the Muslim students. This boosted the MEK's profile and prestige in relation to the secular, Marxist student movements, and deepened the educated younger generation's opposition to the monarchy. While dozens of MEK members were summarily dispatched to face firing squads, appeals from Francois Mitterrand and Jean Paul Sartre persuaded the regime to spare Rajavi from execution. At 24, he was sentenced to life in prison.

From his jail cell, he wrote about the dangers posed by reactionary clerics — an early recognition of Khomeini's political ambition. He authored a book disassociating the MEK from the secular, radical leftists, initially mobilized in sympathy with the MEK dissident movement, who had filled the publicity void beginning in 1972 after the executions of the MEK's leaders and most active members. These doctrinaire Marxist revolutionaries followed a more extremist agenda, murdering Americans while seeking to appropriate the MEK "brand" with names such as 'Mujahidin M.L.' (for Marxist-Leninist), and slightly altered versions of MEK symbols. The split between the 'real' Muslim MEK and the extremist secular splinter group quickly became explicit, then violent. Vahid Afrakhteh, who led the operations to assassinate three U.S. officers in Tehran in 1973 and 1975, also participated in a coup attempt against surviving MEK leaders that killed several of them. One who was targeted and killed in May 1975 by the hard-left splinter group, Majid Sharif-Vaqefi, was later honored for defending Islam; Arya Mehr University of Technology was renamed Sharif University by the mullahs after the revolution, before Rajavi and Khomeini had their fateful falling-out.

While the original MEK had found merit in Marx's analysis of social inequity, they never embraced a Marxist-Leninist political blueprint for governance. A 1984 State Department report to Congress, decades before the derogatory descriptions in vogue today became the norm, described the MEK's founders as *"disaffected young members of the Liberation Movement of Iran, which…initially advocated the use of peaceful means to create a new regime that combined constitutional monarchy with Western European-style socialism."* As a youth movement opposed to the Shah's repression of political dissent and privileging of the country's elite, the MEK attracted people with a range of views, including some hardened radicals and dogmatic leftists. However, the Rajavi-led group that survived and emerged after the revolution — the resistance group that endures today — did not, and does not, hold violence to be a primary means or prerequisite for achieving popular sovereignty in Iran, notwithstanding its period of armed resistance once the clerical regime had begun jailing and executing them indiscriminately as 'enemies of God'.

Interviewed by the French weekly *L'Humanité* on New Year's Day in 1984, Massoud Rajavi said, *"The Islam we profess does not condone bloodshed. We have never sought, nor do we welcome confrontation and violence."* He declared that if Khomeini were prepared to hold *"truly free elections"*, he would return to Iran, and the MEK would *"lay down their arms to participate in such elections."* That offer was not taken up by the clerics.

The NCRI and MEK decided in 2001 to end armed resistance against the regime, and in 2003 handed over all their weaponry to U.S. forces in Iraq. They have long advocated an end to the death penalty in Iran, of which they have almost surely been its most numerous victims since the revolution. In over half a century, although represented in many countries, not once have the NCRI or MEK opened an office in a Communist country. As Rajavi wryly remarked to *Time* magazine in September 1981, *"If Jesus Christ and Mohammed were alive and protesting against Khomeini, he would call them Marxists, too."* And yet, decades later, the 'Marxist' MEK tag endures, recycled under the bylines of American journalists and analysts.

Iran's Post-Revolutionary Future, Briefly Contested

The November 1979 seizure of the American Embassy and ensuing hostage crisis greatly elevated Khomeini politically at the MEK's expense. Prime Minister Bazargan, like Rajavi a political heir to the Mossadeq legacy, immediately resigned in protest. Months before, he and Rajavi had traveled together to Mossadeq's burial site in Ahmad-Abad and spoken at a tribute event. Rajavi ran for President, endorsed by Bazargan among other influential figures, but was banned by Khomeini, as noted. Abolhassan Bani-Sadr, gaining 78.9 percent of the vote, became post-revolutionary Iran's first and only democratically-elected President — every aspirant but Rajavi having appeared on the ballot. (Never again did even 9 percent of registered candidates survive loyalty vetting to appear on the ballot for President; by 2017, the names of more than 99.5 percent of legally registered candidates for President — 1630 out of 1636 — were kept off the ballot.) *Le Monde's* correspondent wrote in March 1980 that had Rajavi been permitted to run, he would likely have received *"several million votes"* with particular support from *"religious and ethnic minorities…a good part of the female vote…and the young."*

A further dispatch at the time from *Le Monde's* Tehran correspondent portrayed a public figure whose description would be unrecognizable to many in Washington today: *"One of the most important events not to be missed in Tehran are the courses on comparative philosophy, taught every Friday afternoon by Mr. Massoud Rajavi. Some 10,000 people presented their admission cards to listen for three hours to the lecture by the leader of the People's Mojahedin on Sharif University's lawn."* His message, the article continued, was that *"freedom is the essence of evolution and the principal message of Islam and revolution."* At one of these lectures, on January 10, 1980, Rajavi said, *"No progress and mobilization for the revolution would be conceivable without guaranteeing freedom for all parties, opinions and writings....We do not accept anything less in the name of Islam."* While Rajavi kept convening large crowds and campaigning publicly for the rights of free speech and assembly, Khomeini sent his loyal enforcers — 'police of the revolution', or *basij* — to disrupt his rallies and attack the MEK's printing presses. Seventy-one MEK members and sympathizers died from such attacks during Iran's fleeting post-revolutionary political season of 1980 and early 1981.

Since the Mossadeq coup of 1953, no moment in Iran's modern history — arguably, not even the hostage crisis — has been more fraught with lasting implications than June 20, 1981, when Iran's political space was, yet again, extinguished, this time with a stunning turn by the regime to bloodshed. Moral judgments have long rested on corrupted accounts of the MEK's resistance to clerical rule. The truth is well-documented: Khomeini and his circle, their primacy threatened by Bani-Sadr's and Rajavi's determined advocacy of democratic rights and the surging popular sentiment behind them, resorted to force.

Earlier in the month, not long after being made commander of the armed forces fighting Iraq, President Bani-Sadr was stripped of his military authority, as Khomeini was organizing loyalists in a Parliament that would support his authority while stepping up repressive measures against others. Massoud Rajavi, seeing the exercise of basic political rights, hard-won in the 1979 revolution, being denied again, proclaimed the people's right to resist by any means. On June 19, 1981, Rajavi called on the population of Iran to turn out *en masse* for a peaceful protest against the assault on their freedoms. The public responded the next day in cities across the country, with a half-million protesting in Tehran alone. Faced with a massive display of public rejection reminiscent of the Shah's final days, Khomeini ordered his security forces to open fire on the crowds. Dozens were killed and thousands arrested. The following day, President Bani-

Sadr was 'impeached' by the mullahs; the Revolutionary Guards seized his residence and closed a newspaper that supported him, imprisoning its writers. They executed three of his closest friends.

June 20, 1981 marked the start of what scholars have termed a "reign of terror" by Khomeini and the Ayatollahs. Since the late 1990s, when the U.S. first designated the MEK and NCRI as terrorists, depictions of Iran's post-revolutionary turn to violence have reflected the regime's 'spin', inverting the accounts commonly seen in earlier years, such as an October 1993 *Associated Press* dispatch that said, *"After the Shah was toppled in 1979, the fundamentalists turned on the Mujahedeen and other leftist and liberal groups who wanted a more secular regime."* Scholars are not wrong to point out the mass appeal that Khomeini had held at the time he returned to Iran, as a seemingly humble, honest figure tapping the public's appetite for a return to Islamic virtues. But the truth is that the mullahs and their supporters, having ridden the Iranian revolution to power, ended up betraying it. They shot their way to power, and since that fateful day in June of 1981, they have relied on lethal force and coercion, not popular will, to maintain it.

The Iran Iraq War and the Fog of History

After Iraq invaded Iran in September 1980, MEK members immediately went to the front lines to defend their country against the Iraqis; many were captured by Iraq and held as prisoners of war (POWs). The fundamentalists, however, not wanting the MEK to gain credit, turned their fighters back. While the conflict was initially, to borrow Richard Haass' terminology, 'a war of necessity' for Iran, after mid-1982 it became 'a war of choice', as Iran had regained all of its territory and had opportunities to end the conflict. In January of 1983, Iraq's Deputy Prime Minister (later Foreign Minister) Tareq Aziz met with Massoud Rajavi in Paris and discussed a settlement of the war. Two months later, the NCRI proposed a UN-led peace initiative including a cease-fire, withdrawal of both sides to the borders previously recognized by both countries in 1975, humane treatment and expeditious exchange of POWs, and negotiation of a peace treaty. Khomeini, however, wanted the war, which he had called *"a gift from God"*. Mediation efforts by others similarly drew no interest from the Supreme Leader. For six more years after expelling Iraq's forces, Khomeini pressed on, using the state of emergency to consolidate absolute control at home.

A common refrain about the MEK heard today is that they betrayed their country by siding with Iraq in the war. Iranians, most of them too young to have experienced the war, have been indoctrinated with this story line, intended to inoculate them from the NCRI and MEK view that their own sacrifices in resisting religious fascism for decades in the face of extreme brutality were nothing if not patriotic. The regime warred against the MEK throughout the 1980s, during which tens of thousands of suspected MEK sympathizers, including many children, were killed by security forces or jailed, tortured and executed. Khomeini's "cultural revolution", purging Iran's higher education establishment, only deepened the alienation of educated youth and their support for the sole resistance group prepared to stand against tyranny. Facing certain death if captured, some MEK members remaining in Iran surreptitiously attacked regime targets; most who made it out of the country regrouped in France.

MEK members were not even present in Iraq for almost six years from the time of Iraq's invasion, and nearly seven years of the war had passed before they had a military capability. Rajavi and about 1,000 MEK individuals relocated to Iraq in June of 1986 after being expelled from France in fulfillment of Khomeini's demand to the government of Prime Minister Chirac, who hoped this would win the freedom of French hostages in Lebanon held by Iran's proxies. Some but not all were released. Saddam Hussein saw the MEK's opposition to Khomeini as an asset and provided excess military hardware to the group. The MEK says it paid Iraq for these weapons in full, in U.S. dollars. The MEK's National Liberation Army (NLA) was announced in June 1987. At no point did the NLA participate in Iraqi combat operations against Iranian forces. The MEK's POWs remained in Iraqi detention along with the other captured Iranian forces until the war's end in 1989 — hardly the treatment Iraq would have accorded a wartime ally.

The NLA's 1988 incursion into Iran — called *Operation Eternal Light* — was not part of the Iran-Iraq war, which by then had reached a cease-fire under UN auspices. While Iraqi aircraft flew partway into Iranian airspace observing the NLA's movement, there was no Iraqi engagement with Iran's forces. The MEK launched this operation convinced that Khomeini and his ruling circle, having depleted the economy, were vulnerable to a popular uprising. However, while regular Iranian Army forces did not put up much resistance, the incursion was halted before reaching Tehran, with mostly IRGC forces and MEK fighters each inflicting heavy casualties on the other. The regime survived.

Tehran's heavily-promoted, heroic rhetoric surrounding the Iraq war is one means of discouraging critical historical scrutiny of Khomeini's role in the conflict, not least its origins. In the months before Saddam invaded, Khomeini had called for Iraqis to overthrow the "non-Islamic" regime in Baghdad led by the "puppet of Satan"; other leading clerics had talked of defeating Saddam Hussein. Khomeini's bid for religious sovereignty over an expansive caliphate encompassing southern Iraq's Shia population — Karbala being designated as the essential waypoint for the revolution to reach Jerusalem (*Qods*) — did not go unnoticed in Baghdad.

Over 90 percent of Iran's war costs and casualties — which by the most conservative estimates numbered 300,000 or more Iranian war dead and many more wounded — were incurred during the years after Iran had regained its territory from Iraq. One day Iranians will be free to engage in critical dialogue about Khomeini's ruinous war policy throughout much of the 1980s.

When Armed Resistance Isn't Terrorism

When that day comes, the fundamentalist clerics will have much to answer for. Only when Tehran's own 'dossier' is exposed in detail will it become clear how the French magistrate, decades later, came to classify all MEK attacks against the regime, including assassinations of notoriously brutal regime figures, as legitimate resistance against tyranny, and not terrorism. For years, until unanimously refuted by multiple judicial reviews during the past decade, western government accounts implied that MEK violence during the 1980s and 1990s had been unprovoked, the expected behavior of extremists and their brainwashed followers. The facts tell a different story.

Now, many governments and the UN are weighing evidence, including recently-disclosed writings and tape recordings, authoritatively confirming that Khomeini ordered the mass execution of as many as 30,000 political prisoners, most of them MEK sympathizers, during the summer and fall of 1988 — a crime against humanity that Geoffrey Robertson, the eminent British human rights lawyer, has equated to the Srebrenica massacre and the Bataan Death March. None had been facing a death sentence, and many had completed their prison sentences.

The total number of NCRI or MEK members and sympathizers killed over the years by the regime may be as high as 100,000. For every man, woman, and child put to death as a member or suspected sympathizer of the MEK, surviving family members carry on, many outside the country. Most are drawn to the NCRI as the one community that understands what they have gone through. That Western analysts and journalists make so little reference to the regime's barbarity aimed at exterminating the MEK, and so readily demean the resistance as a 'cult', misreading the mutual trust on which their very survival depends, as well as the totality of their commitment to see their loved ones' sacrifices validated by ridding Iran of corrupt dictatorship in any form, is a mark of the regime's success in shaping the information domain for so long.

Considering that many reporters and analysts in 2019 still label the MEK and NCRI as the killers of American citizens and Embassy hostage-holders over four decades ago, one would expect anti-MEK opprobrium to have been far more bitter and intense in the immediate aftermath of these and other despicable acts. How curious, then, that Massoud Rajavi would have received letters of admiration and support from major American political figures such as Senator Edward Kennedy, who in June 1984 wrote to the NCRI President lauding the masses of Iranians who had demonstrated on June 20, 1981 in Rajavi's "march for peace and human rights", and claiming that the Iranian people "are being aided by your efforts to promote the goals of peace, democracy and freedom in Iran." Or that then-Congressman John McCain, writing to Rajavi in November of that year, would have said, "I commend you and your compatriots for the courage shown in your endeavor," adding, "The hopes of all Americans for a better Iran are with you."

Eight years later, in 1992 — only months after the MEK, according to the U.S. Counterterrorism Coordinator twenty years later, was said to have "launched near-simultaneous attacks" in 13 countries, including on U.S. soil, and participated in Saddam Hussein's brutal suppression of the national uprising in Iraq's Kurdish north and Shia south — President-elect Bill Clinton saw fit to send Massoud Rajavi a letter at his Paris residence, outlining his intentions to promote democracy movements and soliciting Rajavi's views. The worldwide MEK "attacks" of April 1992 were, in reality, enraged protests by NCRI supporters worldwide following a cross-border Iranian air attack against the resistance based in Iraq, violating the UN-mandated cease-fire, an episode that prompted 230 British Parliamentarians and 219 Members of the U.S. Congress to condemn the government of President Akbar Hashemi Rafsanjani and declare their support for the NCRI. The 2003 U.S. occupation of Iraq, which collected voluminous records from Saddam Hussein's government offices, uncovered no evidence that the MEK had attacked Kurdish or Shia populations, then or at any time.

The way Western journalists and commentators refer to Massoud Rajavi has morphed over time, from prominent political dissident to violent extremist — a terrorist. Actions for which many other anti-regime actors, but not the MEK, were suspected at the time but for which Tehran subsequently chose to blame the MEK, were belatedly added to Western dossiers on the MEK, such as the bombing that killed over 70 key regime figures meeting at the Islamic Republican Party headquarters on June 28, 1981. An exculpatory description of the actual killers of Americans in Iran during the 1970s, after appearing once in the annual U.S. terrorism report on the MEK, disappeared the next year, and thereafter. The question is why — or more to the point, for whose benefit?

To understand how the image of a widely visible and influential Iranian political activist changed after mid-1981, it is instructive to contemplate how his life changed. Before the June 20 crackdown, he led large rallies championing the citizens' "right to demonstrate peacefully". Once the regime launched a manhunt to arrest MEK sympathizers and kill its leaders, Rajavi went into hiding along with ousted President Bani-Sadr, both under MEK protection, and they soon escaped to Paris.

Ashraf Rajavi, Massoud Rajavi's first wife, was killed in Tehran by regime agents in February 1982 along with Moussa Khiabani, a former physics student at the Sharif University of Technology who was considered Rajavi's deputy in the MEK, and his wife. Ashraf's and Massoud's infant son Mostafa survived the gunfire, only to be held above his dead mother's body that evening on state television in a gruesome celebratory tableau. In 1988, the regime killed Rajavi's only sister, Monireh, and her husband. His brother, Ambassador Kazem Rajavi, was assassinated in April 1990 near his home in Geneva. The regime's bombing of Camp Ashraf, Iraq, home to the MEK, with 13 F-4 jets in April 1992, was followed by an official radio announcement in Tehran that the attack had killed Massoud Rajavi, which was untrue, although there was one MEK fatality. The clerics launched SCUD missiles against the MEK in Iraq in 1994 and again in 2001, with the same objective, marking fully twenty years during which Massoud Rajavi was actively targeted for death by regime forces.

As noted, he has not been seen publicly since 2003, although he produced several audio speeches in 2009 that were broadcast on *Simay-e Azadi* (Visage of Freedom) a 24-hour satellite television network associated with the NCRI. Translated excerpts reveal Massoud Rajavi discussing the implications of the MEK's December 2008 removal from the EU terror list. Of particular interest was his encouragement to other parties opposing the clerics' corrupt rule, for example in a July 2009 broadcast during which he criticized the regime's threats to Mir Hossein Moussavi's personal safety following irregularities in the June 2009 presidential elections, which provoked large public protests. Rajavi called for the "illegitimate" elections to be annulled, and for UN monitoring teams to oversee free elections in Iran. These broadcasts were directed to the NCRI and MEK membership. In a lengthy discourse about the MEK's history, Massoud Rajavi stunned many members by declaring a personal commitment that once Iran was ready to conduct free elections, he would exempt himself from participating in any election or holding any government position, stating: *"Membership in the People's Mojahedin, if I were to remain worthy of it, will suffice and is most ideal for me."*

Maryam Rajavi, the current leader of the NCRI ('President-Elect'), is similarly subject to malignant characterizations by many journalists and analysts who either don't know her, are unacquainted with her views, or have nevertheless chosen to hew to the regime's narratives. Born Maryam Qajar-Azodanlu — a descendant of the dynasty that ruled Persia for 136 years until 1925 — she earned a degree in metallurgy from Sharif University. Like so many others in the MEK, her turn to political activism was inspired by first-hand experience of human rights abuses: her sister Narges had been executed by the Shah's security services, while her brother Mahmoud had been imprisoned by the Shah. A champion of women's rights and education, she campaigned for Parliament after the fall of the Shah and won a quarter-million votes, only to be disqualified by Khomeini's political office. A second sister, Massoumeh, was jailed by the mullahs and, along with her husband, tortured to death despite her being eight months pregnant. The mother of an adult daughter, Maryam Rajavi projects compassion and indomitability. Her lifelong determination to defeat religious fascism should surprise no one.

Her demand for women's freedom to choose their own clothing and hold equal rights in marriage, divorce, education and employment, is central to the NCRI-MEK challenge to the regime, a male bastion that has institutionalized misogyny. Her 10-point plan for Iran's future calls for equal participation of women in political leadership, consistent with the rather momentous internal decision the group had made in 1991 to embrace gender equality. Those who know the organization well understand that, in reality, the NCRI and MEK have taken it a step further since then: women hold the leadership positions throughout these organizations and their branch offices. Far from coincidental, this is a direct challenge to the mullahs.

Both the NCRI, headquartered in Paris, and the MEK, now in Albania, are competent, effective organizations. A vibrant, women-led community mobilizing support for political change is more than a rarity in the Muslim world, it is likely unique. With a widening circle of journalists now gaining first-hand knowledge by interviewing MEK and NCRI people — men and women, young and old — toxic caricatures of these people and fanciful descriptions of alleged MEK misdeeds, fed to the media by a handful of one-time MEK members collaborating with Iran's Ministry of Intelligence and Security, are finding a diminishing audience.

Anyone wondering why so many Iranian-Americans, often wearing yellow vests, have shown up just to be seen sitting patiently in congressional hearings on Iran, or standing in the rain for hours bearing signs of protest across the street from the UN when Iranian officials visit New York, need only consider how many exiled Iranians worldwide have suffered the trauma of seeing a parent, sibling, spouse, child or other loved one snatched from their home, incarcerated, tortured, and murdered by this regime. Many surviving family members are permanently separated, unable to reunite in their former homeland, all for the sin of saying no to religious tyranny. Their numbers are not small, and for the NCRI they are a continuous source of support.

Dignitaries and Their Motives

NCRI and MEK members are not the only ones to endure criticism from Washington commentators. Senior ex-officials, civilian and military, and other accomplished Americans, have traveled overseas in recent years to speak at the NCRI's annual rallies, usually held outside of Paris. These individuals, say critics, are making an enormous mistake, allowing themselves to be lured by speakers' fees and lending wholly undeserved prestige and attention to a disreputable group with no possible relevance to the future of Iran.

The huge, teeming exposition hall where rallies have been held, allege the critics, obscures the inconsequential numbers of true NCRI supporters, flanked not only by rented dignitaries from dozens of countries, but also countless busloads of unwitting young people from regions to the east, happy to accept a round trip to France and a stipend just to fill seats stretching to the back reaches of the hall for an afternoon. Critics question the sources of the NCRI's revenue, presuming a dearth of Iranian backers and dependence on external actors with their own agendas, perhaps states hostile to Iran. The resistance, by implication, is not the master of its own house but rather a useful tool for one or another undeclared patron such as the Saudis, Mossad, or even the CIA.

This portrait of the resistance, self-serving for those who repeat it, obscures the reality that the NCRI draws continuous support from a global community of committed Iranians, many inside the country. They watch the pro-NCRI Farsi-language satellite television channel, broadcast from Europe, and donate to its frequent telethons. The demeaning portrayal of American dignitaries attending NCRI rallies flatly misrepresents both what they do with the resistance and why they do it. Whatever speaking fees VIPs may receive for addressing an extraordinarily large audience, streamed by global media outlets and filmed by the NCRI for subsequent viewing in multiple languages, the compensation is no different than what they would command for traveling abroad and delivering a substantive speech to any audience.

What the critics cannot see is the effort expended as many of these Americans stay in regular communication, updating each other about the security of MEK and NCRI members facing constant regime threats and related issues. Some attend less-publicized, or unpublicized, meetings relating to the resistance in the U.S. or Europe. Their private diplomacy, op-eds, media interviews, co-signed letters to government officials expressing policy opinions, and the like are not only uncompensated, but often done without any resistance involvement.

One result is that over time, many journalists and analysts — to say nothing of the U.S. Government — have, by avoiding contact with the NCRI and MEK, ceded to these influential Americans some not insignificant advantages. Many of them have come to know Maryam Rajavi and her circle very well, having held extensive dialogue with them while staying abreast of the NCRI's activities. With years of productive interaction, these former top officials will not be tutored on the nature of the resistance or its leadership by Washington experts who manifestly lack any reliable knowledge of the subject.

Moreover, because the NCRI and MEK, to survive, have had to maintain constant vigilance of Iran's security services, who are even now targeting them for terrorist attack or assassination, the resistance is an unparalleled source of specific information about the regime and its personnel, developed over many years. Former French, German, and Algerian security officials, among others, have touted the NCRI as a source of intelligence. That the U.S. has refrained from establishing a channel of contact with this political opposition group, not even sending a Paris Embassy officer to report on rallies attended by Prime Ministers, Foreign Ministers, parliamentary leaders, and correspondents from dozens of countries, suggests not just an opportunity missed, but a whiff of appeasement.

The Americans who know the NCRI have, between them, listened to the personal accounts of hundreds of members and supporters of the resistance. Each story told puts one more human face on the staggering toll of human rights abuses, transgressions of international laws and norms, and atrocities including crimes against humanity, by the men who have ruled Iran since 1979. The NCRI's trove of documentation on these offenses should, one day, inform an appropriate judicial process of accountability.

An Untold Story, a Higher Calling

There is a reason why a striking array of retired U.S. military officers, representing some of America's most respected senior military leaders and combat veterans of recent years, has made support of the NCRI and MEK a priority over the past decade. They know that Tehran requested and secured a commitment from U.S. envoys in early 2003 to target the MEK as part of the "enemy" during the Iraq intervention that year, while the MEK signaled its neutrality and communicated its locations to the U.S.. The U.S. later confirmed that the MEK was not a combatant during Operation Iraqi Freedom. Camp Ashraf and other MEK sites were bombed anyway by U.S. and British aircraft, killing 50 and wounding many more, according to the resistance. The MEK sought a rendez-vous with American forces and voluntarily turned over all of its weaponry to the U.S. Army 4th Infantry Division. Soon afterward every MEK member submitted to individual interrogation by teams of U.S. intelligence and law enforcement agents. In 2004, fully exonerated from prior transgressions including acts of terrorism, each MEK member signed an agreement and received an identity card from the United States Government marking them all as Protected Persons under the Fourth Geneva Convention.

For five years after the U.S. sent forces into Iraq, with officers assigned to monitor Camp Ashraf, the MEK provided life-saving threat intelligence which helped U.S. forces facing Iraqi insurgent attacks at a time when, as the State Department has recently disclosed, Iran's deadly munitions and proxy militias accounted for over 600 U.S. service members killed and many more wounded. The MEK's wartime cooperation created a bond and a debt of gratitude that a small number of U.S. retired officers have continued to repay with their own considerable support, particularly as the MEK faced mortal threats in Iraq from 2009 to 2016.

An issue of national credibility has motivated many of the American supporters, particularly the retired senior military leaders, overshadowing any concern about facing criticism from Washington bystanders. After U.S. combat forces withdrew from Iraq in 2009, Iraq assumed the American obligation under international law to protect the residents of Camp Ashraf. Iraq breached its obligation, as Iraqi Prime Minister Nouri al-Maliki and President Jalal Talabani chose instead to accommodate Tehran's request to treat the MEK as terrorists and expel them from the country.

What followed was a series of seven lethal attacks over seven years against the entirely defenseless men and women of the MEK. The first two attacks, in 2009 and 2011, were by Iraqi military units associated with the Prime Minister's office, while some others were by Iranian-supported militia, gaining close proximity to the MEK residents by driving vehicles laden with rocket launchers and similar weaponry through access points controlled by Iraqi officers answering to Maliki's office. By the time the surviving MEK residents, relocated at U.S. urging to an austere enclosure near Baghdad Airport called Camp Liberty, had been evacuated to Albania in 2016, over 140 had been killed, seven had been abducted (and not seen since), and more than a thousand had suffered injuries, made worse by delayed, limited or denied access to Iraqi medical treatment.

As Iraq's military, captured on cellphone videos later displayed in congressional hearings, shot at and ran over MEK residents of Camp Ashraf with American-supplied HMMWVs, in blatant violation of Section 3 of the Arms Export Control Act regarding misuse of U.S.-supplied weapons, and clearly exceeding any test for the 'Leahy' prohibitions on training military units engaged in gross human rights abuses, Washington agencies paid no heed. In Europe, on the other hand, the Iraqi Colonel in charge was turned away at the door of the European Parliament, and indicted *in absentia* by a Spanish court.

The most egregious attack occurred on September 1, 2013. An elite Iraqi Army SWAT assault team estimated at 15-20 soldiers, trained in specialized movement and shooting techniques by the U.S., stealthily entered Camp Ashraf, by then inhabited only by a skeleton crew of 100 MEK personnel authorized by the UN to guard the organization's vehicles and equipment after the MEK population had been moved to Camp Liberty. As the MEK cellphone pictures showed, the Iraqi soldiers, their faces masked, bound the wrists of some MEK residents with plastic ties, executing them with pistols muted by silencers, and hunted and killed dozens more among the stay-behind crew. In total, they killed 52 MEK members and abducted seven others, presumably handed over to Iran. The same day, Tehran captured the world media's attention with Foreign Minister Zarif's announcement that President Rouhani would soon travel to New York and address the UN. The September 1 massacre was timed to evade international notice; Iran's readiness to negotiate the future of its nuclear program dominated the news.

To this day, most who blithely criticize former U.S. service chiefs and combatant commanders, CIA and FBI directors, governors, legislators, diplomats, policymakers, a National Security Advisor, an Attorney General and others who have stood with the resistance against such threats, have no conception of the price MEK members have paid in recent years even while assisting and cooperating with the U.S. and relying on its explicit assurance of protection. The UN's human rights officer in Iraq, London-educated Algerian lawyer Tahar Boumedra, resigned from the UNAMI mission in protest of the UN Special Representative's repeated disregard of UN norms in censoring field reports and otherwise concealing from the UN Headquarters Prime Minister Maliki's nefarious collaboration with Tehran against the MEK in Iraq. The UN downplayed Boumedra's detailed, documented allegations but could not rebut them. Secretary of State Hillary Clinton likely never knew, as she pressured the MEK population to relocate from Camp Ashraf to Camp Liberty, that at least five meetings with UNAMI to determine the timing and logistics of the MEK's relocation were held inside Iran's Embassy in Baghdad.

Like the NCRI and MEK members themselves, Americans who have lent their voices to the resistance-led call for a free Iran exhibit no reticence, embarrassment, or doubt that their actions reflect enduring principles long held to be important by the U.S.. For the military veterans in particular — acutely mindful of the U.S. commitments made to the MEK residents in Iraq, and the repeated deadly attacks that followed — it is a matter of honor.

Who Should be Criticizing Whom?

Some Iran-watchers who have hoped for U.S. rapprochement with Tehran and lamented the recent downturn in bilateral relations will have assumed from the title alone that the author's intent is to promote the NCRI as a successor government to the clerical regime. In Washington circles, such a Pavlovian leap of logic is not unusual, wherein the mere mention of the MEK or NCRI prompts a quick admonition that one is obviously ignorant of political sentiment among the Iranian population, and that the NCRI and MEK hold no place in an informed conversation about who might lead a 'reformed' Iran.

That would be a misreading of this essay. Although many of the American and foreign dignitaries who address NCRI rallies do indeed believe, and say, that the organized resistance would be infinitely preferable to the current rulers and should be supported, and NCRI representatives habitually describe the resistance as a democratic alternative to the current dictatorship, the formal NCRI policy prescription is a blueprint for popular sovereignty and democratic legitimacy in Iran. From the first time the author heard Maryam Rajavi address her supporters, in June 2011, she has consistently made clear that the goal of the NCRI is to deliver self-determination to the Iranian people, facilitating a transparent roadmap leading to a government mandated by the votes of every man and woman under a new constitution.

In this *"free and democratic republic"*, said Mrs. Rajavi at that rally, marking thirty years since Khomeini's reign of terror began, *"we would be content to remain in opposition and feel honored to sacrifice ourselves for the sake of giving the Iranian people the ability to choose freely"*. Her position echoed that of Massoud Rajavi decades earlier, interviewed in Paris on January 9, 1982. As he told an Iranian Muslim students' journal, *"It is not enough to have gone through the trials of repression, imprisonment, torture, and execution under the Shah and the mullahs. The Mujahedeen must also pass the test of general elections."*

No, the purpose here is not to preempt Iranian citizens' choices on who will lead their country — that has been done quite enough since 1906 — nor even to offer an opinion from afar, but to address a serious national security concern about the parameters of the U.S. policy debate on Iran. This concern comes into sharp focus with a more accurate, granular understanding of who the MEK are, and what happened between the regime and the resistance from the time of the revolution. The implications of that revealed history are profound not only for Tehran, but for Washington.

Consider how American principles and interests factor into the Iran conversation in Washington. A durable constituency continues to repose its hopes in President Rouhani, apparently believing that his vision for Iran is defined by a readiness to engage peacefully with the world if only Iran's interests are respected. And yet, has this proposition not already been tested? More than a decade ago, Secretary of State Condoleezza Rice, writing in *Foreign Affairs*, suggested that *"Iran must make a strategic choice….Does it want to continue thwarting the legitimate demands of the world, advancing its interests through violence…? Or is it open to a better relationship, one of growing trade and exchange, deepening integration, and peaceful cooperation with its neighbors and the broader international community?"*

Clearly, Iran's nuclear diplomacy, conducted over two years with the P5+1 in a congenial atmosphere and producing an agreement in 2015, led many Americans to assume that it had made the strategic choice described by Secretary Rice, deciding to follow the more cooperative path. No questions were raised about the 'moderate' Rouhani's choice in 2013 of Hossein Dehghan to be his Defense Minister — the man who, as an IRGC officer in 1982-83, had organized the initial training of the new Hizballah militia in Lebanon and overseen the bombing of the U.S. Marine Barracks that killed 241 servicemen including 220 Marines. (Dehghan was replaced after President Trump took office and staffed three top positions with Marine Generals.)

No concern was expressed about his Minister of Justice, Mostafa Pourmohammadi, who had been one of three regime officials on the Tehran 'death panel' personally assigning death sentences to many of the 30,000 political prisoners during the 1988 massacre, a second of the three being the recently-appointed Chief Justice of Iran and 2017 Presidential candidate, Ebrahim Raisi. The current Justice Minister, Alireza Avayi, served on a similar panel in Khuzistan Province. There are others implicated in that infamous crime who today hold positions of authority.

The fact that nearly 4,000 internationally-documented executions with no due process have taken place under the Rouhani Presidency since 2013 — the highest per-capita rate of executions in the world — is all but lost in the veritable avalanche of regime transgressions. No other government in the world has so degraded international security, from commanding tens of thousands of ground forces facilitating the Assad regime's catastrophic destruction of cities and towns across Syria, displacing eleven million citizens and killing hundreds of thousands, to conducting terrorist operations in several European countries and beyond while abusing diplomatic cover, pursuing escalatory ballistic missile development, arming and funding proxy militias fomenting sectarian strife in neighboring countries, helping the Houthis launch well over 200 missiles against populated areas in Saudi Arabia, and mounting operations in southern Syria that increasingly threaten Israel's security. Tehran's rampant corruption, environmental neglect, trafficking in persons, international drug trafficking, money laundering, and other manifestations of perverse, neglectful governance, have been downplayed and might have been ignored altogether had protests not erupted across Iran beginning in late December 2017.

Who could fault Rouhani for expecting the Washington commentariat to nod their heads in agreement when his September 21, 2018 op-ed in the *Washington Post* referred to *"our tradition of respect for the rule of law and norms of international law"* and desire *"to safeguard peace and security in the region"*? Or Foreign Minister Mohammed Javad Zarif for chuckling to himself as he chides the U.S. for its historic guilt in having engineered the 1953 coup against Mossadeq? His American friends, ever keen to score that next interview, seem unaware that the leading clerics at that time, including Ayatollahs Behbehani, Kashani, and Khomeini's mentor Borujerdi, all supported the coup and the Shah's return to power. They wanted Mossadeq to receive — what else? — the death penalty. Zarif's admirers in Washington, by challenging any hint of favorable consideration of the NCRI and its positions, have done their part to assure the continued exclusion of Mossadeq's influence from the Iran policy discussion — perpetuating Operation Ajax, as it were, 66 years after the fact.

The Trump Administration, while not indicating any favor toward the NCRI, has faced criticism not only for pulling out of the JCPOA, but for setting what some regard as an unrealistically high 'bar' for Tehran to meet if it is to gain relief from the Administration's "maximum pressure" campaign. Secretary Pompeo's 12 demands ask a lot from Iran. But which among them would critics be content to take off the table: Keep the American and allied hostages? Continue shielding its nuclear files, uninspected sites, and enrichment capabilities? Maintain support for terrorist groups and Shia proxy militias? Keep up the ballistic missile attacks and destabilizing meddling in the Levant and the Gulf?

In Washington, politicians and analysts who lack faith, if they ever had it, in the regime's 'reformists' to deliver Iran and the world from the four-decade geopolitical nightmare hatched by Khomeini and his divine constitutional writ are listened to, if tacitly disdained, by the establishment. Yet prominent figures who travel overseas and stand with the NCRI are vilified. And what exactly are the policies these dignitaries have had the shameless temerity to endorse?

There are ten: universal suffrage, respect for individual freedoms and universal access to the internet, an end to the death penalty, separation of religion and state and an end to religious discrimination, "complete gender equality" including "equal participation of women in political leadership", abolition of

Sharia law and institution of an independent judiciary with due process and the presumption of innocence, commitment to international conventions upholding human rights and the equality of all nationalities, protection of property rights in a free-market economy along with environmental conservation, peaceful coexistence with other countries with respect for the UN Charter, and a non-nuclear Iran free of weapons of mass destruction. Maryam Rajavi has tirelessly advocated this ten-point plan for many years, to every audience and in every language. There is no hidden agenda.

Glass Houses and Undeclared Motives

Something is deeply amiss in the Washington policy discussion of Iran. The case for re-joining the JCPOA and hoping that non-nuclear concerns will be satisfactorily addressed through positive engagement with Tehran is ever-harder to make, as the level of realpolitik implied finds ever less mooring in American principles. At the same time, the basis for continuing to treat the NCRI and MEK as if they do not exist, and have had no role either in the history of post-revolutionary Iran or in the regime's current travails, has collapsed, as Tehran's fabrications have been exposed. The decades-long regime strategy to deny any credibility to the 'MKO terrorist grouplet' has come undone, as leading clerics, including Supreme Leader Ali Khamenei, now openly decry the MEK's role in coordinating protests within cities and towns across Iran. Iranian intelligence has been repeatedly caught generating counterfeit information under cover of trusted western academic, media and NGO institutions. Reporters formerly working for Iran's state-run media have migrated overseas and resurfaced in what Professor Ivan Sascha Sheehan terms Tehran's *"plan to plant its apologists in Western newsrooms."*

Officials and legislators in Europe and Canada have already factored the historical distortions, false narratives, and judicial exonerations of the MEK into their policies and dealings with Tehran. President Macron's refusal of Rouhani's January 2018 request to take action against the Paris-based NCRI for fomenting the protests inside Iran is but one example.

In the U.S., however, illusions live on. Even if, as critics are quick to claim, the resistance lacks popular support inside Iran, there would be no way for an objective pollster to 'control' for the fact that under the Islamic Punishment Act, which is the current penal code, anyone overheard expressing a favorable view of the NCRI or MEK is subject to amputation, hanging, execution, or if the religious judge is lenient, exile. It should not be necessary to point out that any polling organization functioning in Iran exists to serve the regime's goal of retaining power. In any case, while it is fair game for Washington analysts to speculate about who might find favor with 80 million Iranians, the NCRI is the only voice advocating a process to find out.

Although protests throughout Iran have continued well into their second year despite harsh reprisals, in Washington it is still *de rigeur* among analysts and correspondents to opine that the Tehran regime faces no serious danger of collapse. Such an assessment overlooks the fact that the long-term survival of blood-stained autocracies has been more the exception than the rule in the post-Cold War era. There being other possibilities, betting on the perpetuation of clerical dictatorship in Iran not only risks strategic surprise, it waives any claim to be the more morally-grounded view, if it ever was.

This is not to argue for turning the tables and trying to silence the NCRI's critics; they are free to express their views. But those who have raised the issue of motives, incentives and unseen influences in pointing to the NCRI's supporters should have no objection to having their own circumstances similarly scrutinized. Assuming those interested in Iran policy can all agree on the preferability of an intellectually uncorrupted debate, there should be no basis for selectively excluding pertinent facts. Above all, it is imperative — and long overdue — to assure Americans that the regime in Tehran is not exerting unseen influence on the nation's foreign policy.

Some whose bylines have repeatedly carried allegations that the NCRI and MEK constitute a terrorist cult will be loath to acknowledge that these themes have been debunked, having invested their credibility in that portrayal. Others, reporters and journalists whose professional stature has been enhanced by interviewing senior Iranian officials, face a similar quandary, knowing that to report truthfully about the NCRI will be to burn their bridges with the regime. This is particularly the case with newspapers and media organizations who would be risking the wholesale denial of access to Iran and its officials. To apply high journalistic standards in reporting on the NCRI or MEK is to enter a minefield. Should readers not be made aware of the self-censorship at play?

With American officials shut out of Iran for the past four decades, demand for Farsi language training has been low, but many outstanding Iranian-Americans with language fluency and a superior understanding of Iranian culture and politics have supported the policy process from inside and outside the government. With their former homeland in the grip of dictatorship, Iranian-Americans appreciate guaranteed freedoms in the U.S. more than most. That having been said, the regime is known to coerce resident citizens to influence the activities of their relatives abroad. During the Cold War, the U.S. paid close attention to similar tactics at play within America's ethnic populations from "captive nations". Are there no grounds for concern with Iran today?

The author's 2013 study of allegations regarding the MEK, reviewing 19 consecutive versions of the State Department's annual *Country Reports on Terrorism*, revealed highly irregular, indeed flagrantly erratic, editorial alterations of the MEK's alleged terrorist history, from one version to the next. Clearly this was no accident; how did it happen?

The Alavi Foundation, originally created by the Shah in 1973, has donated large sums to many of America's top universities among other charitable activities aimed, it says, at promoting understanding of Persian culture. One university receiving its grant funding hosts a policy program that for years has widely disseminated defamatory dispatches about the MEK, entirely uncorroborated, from a notorious MOIS agent in Europe who left the MEK many years ago. The Manhattan Prosecutor's office uncovered illicit banking connections over a decade ago tying the Alavi Foundation to the Iranian government, and in 2017 the Southern District of New York won a major federal case confirming that the Alavi Foundation is in fact a front for Iran.

Leading universities have provided a distinguished perch for former regime members now resident in the U.S. These include an outspoken former Iranian Ambassador who, 22 years ago, was recalled to Tehran before the German government could expel him for his Embassy's role as a conduit for regime operatives who opened fire with machine guns in a Berlin restaurant in September 1992, killing four Iranian Kurdish dissident leaders.

In 2002, while pro-NCRI Iranian-Americans were taking care to avoid being accused of materially supporting an organization on the terrorism list, an Iranian founded an organization in the U.S. presenting itself as the voice of Iranian-Americans. Given his impressive access to senior Iranian officials over the ensuing years, Americans could be forgiven for assuming this was a hopeful signal of Iranian goodwill toward the United States. Over a decade later, when a Comedy Central host prompted the individual to admit that he held Iranian but not U.S. citizenship, it was not clear that he had ever disclosed to his

Iranian-American constituents that their founder and leader was not an Iranian-American. Leading American newspapers continue to cite him as a primary source of insight on policy choices facing the U.S.

How many red flags are needed to justify a proper counter-intelligence investigation?

Russian intelligence pursues America's military secrets and seeks to undermine U.S. political and social cohesion. Chinese intelligence targets America's advanced industrial and digital technologies. But Iran's security institutions exist for one purpose only: to keep the regime from falling. In the United States, that means sustaining influence operations aimed at dissuading the U.S. from policies that would exploit the regime's political illegitimacy, embolden its domestic detractors, blunt its regional destabilization activity, react forcefully to its terrorism and aggression, and — the threat it has spared no effort to block — afford the organized political resistance a greater opportunity to be heard.

When — not if — Maryam Rajavi travels to the U.S. one day, the 'terrorist-Marxist-traitor-cult' melody will be heard again; but that will be its swan song. The community for whom she speaks, including many tens of thousands no longer alive to testify; the road they have traveled; the tests they have survived; and the reasons they carry on, will at last dispel Washington's serial misunderstanding of the resistance.

No longer will the regime be able to rub out — like an altered photograph of Soviet leaders atop Lenin's Mausoleum — its place in the Iranian people's more than century-long battle for their future. No longer will it be possible for correspondents or policy analysts to conform to Tehran's tacit parameters without the extent of their compromised professional standards being apparent. As with Russia's meddling in U.S. elections, Iran's meddling in U.S. policy deliberations will merit serious national reflection.

Then, it is to be hoped, the U.S. foreign policy community can engage in a debate on Iran free of outside influence, a debate more reliably grounded in facts, interests, principles and strategic priorities — the kind of debate, in other words, that has always enabled America to find consensus, address the hardest international challenges and, in time, surmount them.

About the Author

LINCOLN BLOOMFIELD JR. served in five previous administrations under three Presidents. He was U.S. Special Envoy for MANPADS Threat Reduction from 2008–09 with the rank of Ambassador. From 2001–2005 he was Assistant Secretary of State for Political Military Affairs, also serving as Special Representative of the President and Secretary of State for Humanitarian Mine Action. He was Deputy Assistant Secretary of State for Near Eastern Affairs (1992–93), Deputy Assistant to the Vice President for National Security Affairs (1991–92), member of the U.S. team negotiating for U.S. facilities in the Philippines (1991–92) and the U.S. water mediation between Israel and Jordan (1990), and Principal Deputy Assistant Secretary of Defense for International Security Affairs (1988–89) among other policy positions in the Department of Defense beginning in 1981. Ambassador Bloomfield served for eight years until 2017 as Chairman of the non-partisan Stimson Center in Washington, and now serves as Chairman Emeritus and Distinguished Fellow. He is a National Executive Committee Member of the U.S. Water Partnership and a Director of the non-profit energy NGO The Last Kilometer, along with several commercial engagements. Author of *The Mujahedin-e Khalq — MEK: Shackled by a Twisted History* (University of Baltimore, 2013) among other writings, and a frequent commentator on foreign policy and national security issues, he is a graduate of Harvard College (*a.b.*) and the Fletcher School of Law and Diplomacy (M.A.L.D.).

Additional writings and testimony by the author on this subject may be accessed at these links:

The Mujahedin-e Khalq — MEK: Shackled by a Twisted History: https://www.amazon.com/Mujahedin-Khalq-Shackled-Twisted-History/dp/0615783848

"Mujahedin-e Khalq (MEK/PMOI) and the Search for Ground Truth About its Activities and Nature — An Independent Assessment", *http://palmercoates.com/wordpress/wp-content/uploads/2016/09/MEK-PMOI-and-the-Search-for-Ground-Truth-about-its-Activities-and-Nature-1.pdf*

Prepared testimony for hearing before the House Committee on Foreign Affairs, Subcommittee on Oversight and Investigations and Subcommittee on the Middle East and South Asia "Camp Ashraf: Iraqi Obligations and State Department Accountability," December 7, 2011: *http://palmercoates.com/wordpress/wp-content/uploads/2016/10/Dec-7-2011-Camp-Ashraf-HFAC.pdf*

Prepared testimony for hearing before the House Committee on Foreign Affairs, Subcommittee on Oversight and Investigations "Conditions at Camp Liberty: U.S. and Iraqi Failures," September 13, 2012: *http://palmercoates.com/wordpress/wp-content/uploads/2016/10/Sept-13-2012-HASC-Sctee-Oversight-and-Investigations.pdf*

www.ingramcontent.com/pod-product-compliance
Lightning Source LLC
Chambersburg PA
CBHW041302040426
42334CB00028BA/3126